AN OLD FASHIONED CHRISTMAS

BY PAUL ENGLE

Poetry

WORN EARTH
AMERICAN SONG
CORN
WEST OF MIDNIGHT
AMERICAN CHILD (1945)
AMERICAN CHILD (enlarged edition, 1956)
THE WORD OF LOVE
POEMS IN PRAISE

Novel

ALWAYS THE LAND

Opera Libretto

GOLDEN CHILD

Reminiscences

A PRAIRIE CHRISTMAS

AN OLD FASHIONED CHRISTMAS

by Paul Engle

Illustrated by Eleanor Pownall Simmons.

THE DIAL PRESS NEW YORK  1964

LIBRARY OF CONGRESS CATALOG CARD NUMBER: 64-19934

SECOND PRINTING

DESIGNED BY ALAN MICHAEL HEICKLEN
MANUFACTURED IN THE UNITED STATES OF AMERICA

This book about the most special day in our year is dedicated to Pauline V. Moore, M. D., of Iowa City, who dedicates herself every day in the year.

ACKNOWLEDGMENTS

The author wishes to acknowledge the generous help of Ada Stoflet, University of Iowa Library, who makes that place into a holiday of books.

Some of this material, in a rather different form, was first published through the Register & Tribune Syndicate, Des Moines, Iowa. Thanks are due to Frank Eyerly, Bruce Horton and Kenneth MacDonald, who keep the state of Iowa aware of its old fashions as well as its new. Thanks are due, too, to Longman's, Green & Co., Inc. for permission to use material which first appeared, in different form, in *Prairie Christmas.* Sonnet XXVIII is reprinted from *American Child,* copyright 1954, 1956 by Paul Engle and published by The Dial Press.

Some of the material was written at the urging of Curtiss Anderson, one of the best magazine editors in the business, while he was associated with The Meredith Publishing Co. of Des Moines, Iowa. It was later edited, to its great benefit, by Mr. Anderson, assisted by Gordon Greer. Both had just the right and warm feeling for this account of an event in the cold season.

TABLE OF CONTENTS

AN OLD FASHIONED CHRISTMAS

A Christmas Child

Hearing about those winter nights
When Mary traveled to that place
And had her Child, our own child's face
Illuminates the Christmas lights.
She shudders with that desert cold,
As if she, also, huddled there
When the Child breathed His first live air,
Eternally but one day old.

I'd help, she cries, I'd give my coat,
The one that's trimmed with rabbit fur,
My muff and mittens. As her throat
Pulses in pride and love, the wild
And mortal childhood live in her
Praises that calm, immortal Child.

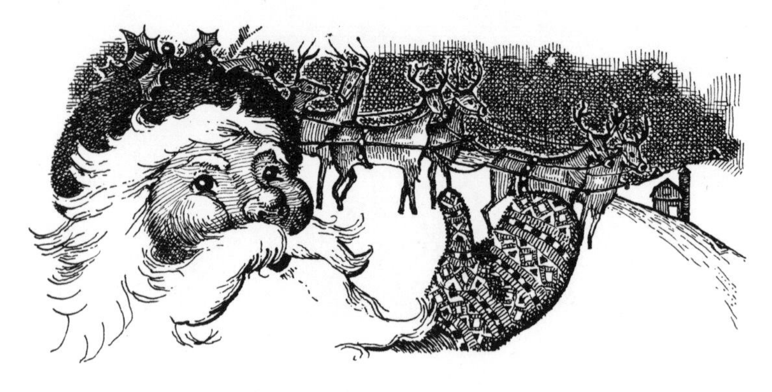

The Merry Holiday

Fourth of July is fire and bang,
The high-exploding rocket,
Saved pennies, until they are spent,
Burning the small boy's pocket.

Thanksgiving is the time we praise
The tasting tongue, the belly,
The turkey dripping with its juice,
The clear crabapple jelly.

But Christmas is the holiday
When all our faces carry
A look of joy, and all our mouths
Utter the one word—*merry.*

An Iowa Christmas

very Christmas should begin with the sound of bells, and when I was a child mine always did. But they were sleigh bells, not church bells, for we lived in a part of Cedar Rapids, Iowa, where there were no churches. My bells were on my father's team of horses as he drove up to our horse-headed hitching post with the bobsled that would take us to celebrate Christmas on the family farm ten miles out in the country. My father would bring the team down Fifth Avenue at a smart trot, flicking his whip over the horses' rumps and making the bells double their light, thin jangling over the snow, whose radiance threw back a brilliance like the sound of bells.

Whose father now drives up on Christmas morning in such exciting style as mine did when I was a child?

With more anticipation than we would have today waiting for a jet to fly in from Paris, my younger sister and I would stand at a window looking down the street. Kathryn would clap her hands, jump up and down, and cry "There he comes!"

Such speed, such power, it seemed, such a roar of arrival with the runners crunching on the snow, the bells clanging, the horses snorting as father snapped his long whip over their heads! How dull the rubber-skidded arrival of a plane, compared to the rush and clang of steel runners beautifully sliding over ice and snow.

Father would bring the bobsled smartly around in a whirl of snow and prancing feet in the sort of arrival which no plane on a runway and no car on a plowed and paved street could ever imitate. By then my sister and I would have run out to help, holding the reins between us as father tied the team to our hitching post. There was more feeling of motion and flight in our two horsepower, Billy and Buck, than in any hundreds of mechanical horsepower.

Our whole Christmas was that way; there was more life in it, close to animals and to the land, than in our city celebration today. Like most people toward the beginning of this troubled century, we had relatives on the farm.

There are no such departures as ours for that farm any more: the whole family piling into the bobsled with a foot of golden oat straw to lie in and heavy buffalo robes to lie under, the horses stamping the soft snow, and at every motion of their hoofs the bells jingling, jingling. My father sat there with the reins firmly held, wearing a long coat made from the hide of a favorite family horse, the deep chestnut color still glowing, his mittens also from the same hide. It always troubled me as a boy of eight that the horses had so indifferent a view of their late friend appearing as a warm overcoat on the back of the man who put the iron bit in their mouths.

A bobsled was the wonderful and proper way to travel on Christmas morning. The space it offered was generous, like the holiday itself. There was no crowding on narrow seats where children had to sit upright. Instead, the long, wide body allowed us such comfort and freedom as no car or plane can give.

In that abundant dimension, we could burrow down under the clean-smelling straw, pull a shaggy robe over us, and travel warm and snug while still being outdoors with the wind in our faces.

We could hop out and ride on the heavy runners, the snow piling up against our boots and the runners making it seem dangerous as they bounced and twisted over the unpaved streets, making their hissing, tearing sound over the packed snow.

It was a close and intimate Christmas, and like that whole feeling of warm familiarity was the sound of the bobsled's runners. Their expressive noise is gone forever, and no rubber tire hissing on pavement can ever have such exciting variety.

As the runners slid over snow, ice, and an occasional stone or bare spot with dirt, they would carry on a sustained monologue continually changing. They would whisper gently over snow, mutter angrily over ice, squeak over gravel, cry in rage over an exposed rock, then go back to the long rhythm of the glide over hard-packed snow.

That was dramatic travel, just as the horses, alive and individual, each with its own characteristics, were a more exciting source of motive power than a mechanical engine with its stink and noise.

We were close to those horses. My father had bought them young and trained them himself, so that he could drive them with a light hand, as much by the expressive sound of his voice as by a whip on the withers or a bit in the mouth. We would continually urge Billy along as he lagged just enough behind Buck so that he had a little less to pull.

On a level piece of road, Father would collect the reins firmly, cluck to the team, snap the whip over their ears, and settle them into a fast trot, bells jangling in celebration, runners clacking, and the children yelling with the speed and sway of it.

There are no streets like those any more: the snow sensibly left on the road for the sake of sleighs and easy travel. And along the streets we met other horses, so that we moved from one set of bells to another, from the tiny tinkle of the individual bells on the shafts to the silvery, leaping sound of the long strands hung over the harness. There would be an occasional brass-mounted automobile laboring on its narrow tires and as often as not pulled up the slippery hills by a horse, and we would pass it with a triumphant shout for an awkward nuisance which was obviously not here to stay.

The country road ran through a landscape of little hills and shallow valleys and heavy groves of timber, including one of great towering black walnut trees which were all cut down a year later to be made into gunstocks for the First World War. The great moment was when we left the road and turned up the long lane on the farm. It ran through fields where watermelons were always planted in the summer because of the fine sandy soil, and I could go out and break one open to see its Christmas colors of green skin and red inside. My grandfather had been given some of that farm as bounty land for service as a cavalryman in the Civil War.

My uncle, mother's brother, and our cousins lived on the same place where mother had been born. Somehow, a place of country quiet, with livestock crunching on its feed, with sheds and barns and corncribs, with crop and pasture land rolling away serenely, their shape clearer in winter under the defining snow, seemed the best of all possible places to celebrate this holiday begun in a little village in sheepraising country on the other side of the world.

Near the low house on the hill, with oaks on one side and apple trees on the other, my father would stand up, flourish his whip, and bring the bobsled right up to the door of the house with a burst of speed.

There are no such arrivals any more: the harness bells ringing and clashing, the horses whinnying at the horses in the barn and receiving a great, trumpeting whinny in reply, the dogs leaping into the bobsled and burrowing under the buffalo robes, a squawking from the hen house, a yelling of "Whoa, whoa," at the excited horses, boy and girl cousins howling around the bobsled, and the descent into the snow with the Christmas basket carried by my mother.

My Uncle Charlie was certainly not John the Baptist wearing a coat of camel's hair and a leather girdle about his loins. Nor was he preaching "Repent ye: for the kingdom of heaven is at hand."

But standing at the farmhouse door, wearing a heavy sheepskin jacket over his stained overalls, urging us in with a hearty shout of, "Come and set where it's warm," he was certainly a prophet. What he prophesied was good cheer and a gay Christmas.

Charlie had the gentle disposition of a saint and the shoulders of a professional wrestler. He had once stayed five minutes in a ring at the county fair with a champion known with cruel candor as "The Strangler."

As I went in, he would give my arm a friendly twist and say in great confidence, lowering his voice to make me feel that I too was a pretty good country wrestler, "After dinner we'll go down to the haymow and I'll show you how to break out of a hammer lock."

After mother, the girls and the baskets had been rushed into the house by our cousins, and the dogs persuaded out of the straw, we would go on to the barn. Charlie would help father unhitch the team and take them into stalls, where they could see the horses which had been whinnying at them in suspicious welcome.

A barn was the most wonderful place for a child to begin Christmas Day, the same sort of place where that first Day took place. Here were the snorts and stampings and mutterings of livestock, the yowling of cats waiting for the saucer of milk. It was a modest barn, but rich with abundant life, and the mangers were filled with nourishment for that life.

The children of those countries which celebrate it are fortunate to have Christmas, but I was lucky beyond most children to have my day begin at a cheerful barn on a low hill in the prairie, where the animals and I could look across the snowy country and be glad we were inside.

That winter odor of a barn is a wonderfully complex one, rich and warm and utterly unlike the smell of the same barn in summer: the body heat of many animals weighing a thousand pounds and more; pigs in one corner making their dark, brown-sounding grunts; milk cattle still nuzzling the manger for wisps of hay; horses eying the newcomers and rolling their deep, oval eyes white; oats, hay, and straw tangy still with the live August sunlight; the manure steaming; the sharp odor of leather harness rubbed with neat's-foot oil to keep it supple; the molasses-sweet odor of ensilage in the silo where the fodder was almost fermenting. It is a smell from strong and living things, and my father always said it was the secret of health, that it scoured out a man's lungs; and he would stand there, breathing deeply, one hand on a horse's rump, watching the steam come out from under the blankets as the team cooled down from their rapid trot up the lane. It gave him a better appetite, he argued, than plain fresh air, which was thin and had no body to it.

By the time we reached the house my mother and sisters were wearing aprons and busying in the kitchen, as red-faced as the women who had been there all morning. The kitchen was the biggest room in the house and all family life save sleeping went on there. The kitchen range was a tremendous black and gleaming one called a Smoke Eater, with pans bubbling over the holes above the firebox and a reservoir of hot water at the side, lined with dull copper, from which my uncle would dip a basin of water and shave above the sink, turning his lathered face now and then to drop a remark into the women's talk, waving his straight-edged razor as if it were a threat to make them believe him. My job was to go to the woodpile out back and keep the fire burning, splitting the chunks of oak and hickory, watching how cleanly the ax went through the tough wood.

The Tree

Now in the white
Winter of snowing
We get our tree:
Green hue of growing.

It comes to stay
With us inside,
To be green life
In its green pride.

Now at the sleepy
End of year,
It lives with us
For our green cheer.

On the Farm

he tree was brought out from town, and on it were many paper ornaments made by my cousins, as well as beautiful ones brought from the Black Forest, where the family had originally lived. There were popcorn balls, from corn planted on the sunny slope next to the watermelons, paper horns with homemade candy, and apples from the orchard. The gifts tended to be hand-knit socks, or wool ties, or fancy crocheted "yokes" for nightgowns, tatted collars for blouses, doilies with fancy flower patterns for tables, tidies for chairs, and once I received a brilliantly polished cow horn with a cavalryman crudely but bravely carved on it. And there would usually be a cornhusk doll, perhaps with a prune or walnut for a face, and a gay dress of old corset-cover scrap with its ribbons still bright. And there were real candles burning with real flames, every guest sniffing the air for the smell of scorching pine needles. No electrically lit tree has the warm and primitive presence of a tree with a crown of living fires over it, suggesting whatever true flame Joseph may have kindled on that original cold night.

There are no dinners like that any more: every item from the farm itself, with no deep-freezer, no car for driving into town for packaged food. The pies had been baked the day before, pumpkin, apple, and mince; as we ate them, we could look out the window and see the cornfield where the pumpkins grew, the trees from which the apples were picked. There was cottage cheese, with the dripping bags of curds still hanging from the cold cellar ceiling. The bread had been baked that morning, heating up the oven for the meat, and as my aunt hurried by I could smell in her apron the freshest of all odors with which the human nose is honored—bread straight from the oven. There would be a huge brown crock of beans with smoked pork from the hog butchered every November. We would see, beyond the crock, the broad black iron kettle in a corner of the barnyard, turned upside down, the innocent hogs stopping to scratch on it.

There would be every form of preserve; wild grape from the vines in the grove, crabapple jelly, wild blackberry and tame raspberry, strawberry from the bed in the garden, sweet and sour pickles with dill from the edge of the lane where it grew wild, pickles from the rind of the same watermelon we had cooled in the tank at the milkhouse and eaten on a hot September afternoon.

Cut into the slope of the hill behind the house, with a little door of its own, was the vegetable cellar, from which came carrots, turnips, cabbages, potatoes, squash. Sometimes my scared cousins were sent there for punishment, to sit in darkness and meditate on their sins; but never on Christmas Day. For days after such an ordeal, they could not endure biting into a carrot.

And of course there was the traditional sauerkraut, with flecks of caraway seed. I remember one Christmas Day, when a ten-gallon crock of it in the basement, with a stone weighting down the lid, had blown up, driving the stone against the floor of the parlor, and my uncle had exclaimed, "Good, God, the piano's fallen through the floor."

All the meat was from the home place too. Turkey, of course, and most useful of all, the goose—the very one which had chased me the summer before, hissing and darting out its bill at the end of its curving neck like a feathered snake. Here was the universal bird of an older Christmas: its down was plucked, washed, and hung in bags in the barn to be put into pillows; its awkward body was roasted until the skin was crisp as a fine paper; and the grease from its carcass was melted down, a little camphor added, and rubbed on the chests of coughing children. We ate, slept on, and wore that goose.

The most tantalizing odor of all was the sour goose. This was an old family tradition brought from Germany, and was Charlie's favorite eating. For many families the typical tone of Christmas was the sweetness of cake and candy. For us, it was the splendid sourness of vinegar poured over a cooking goose, the acid fumes tickling our delighted noses.

This was Aunt Minnie's specialty, I suppose because she seemed to have as much vinegar in her veins as blood, and a tongue as sharp as the fork with which she tested the goose.

Minnie was thin and sharp in her features, too, and I can see her bending over that plump goose and stabbing it with her fork to see whether the skin was crisp, almost as if she resented any creature which was so fat it made her own skinniness more apparent. In the bottom of the pan, vinegar and grease bubbled happily together, Minnie scooping up the pungent broth and basting the goose with it.

When serving the sour goose, Charlie would put a large piece on my plate and say, "Eat hearty, boy, that goose will put wire in your muscles."

I believed him, and I bit into the meat with its biting taste. In a few years Charlie was gone, there was no more sour goose, and my muscles have been softer ever since.

I was blessed as a child with a remote uncle from the nearest railroad town, Uncle Ben, who was admiringly referred to as a "railroad man," working the run into Omaha.

Ben had been to Chicago; just often enough, as his wife Minnie said with a sniff in her voice, "to ruin the fool, not often enough to teach him anything useful." Ben refused to eat fowl in any form, and as a Christmas token a little pork roast would be put in the oven just for him, always referred to by the hurrying ladies in the kitchen as "Ben's chunk." Ben would make frequent trips to the milkhouse, returning each time a little redder in the face, usually with one of the men toward whom he had jerked his head. It was not many years before I came to associate Ben's remarkably fruity breath not only with the mince pie, but with the jug I found sunk in the bottom of the cooling tank with a stone tied to its neck. He was a romantic person in my life for his constant travels and for that dignifying term "railroad man," so much more impressive than farmer or lawyer. Yet now I see that he was a short man with a fine natural shyness, giving us knives and guns because he had no children of his own.

And of course the trimmings were from the farm too: the hickory nut cake made with nuts gathered in the grove after the first frost and hulled out by my cousins with yellowed hands; the black walnut cookies, sweeter than any taste; the fudge with butternuts crowding it. In the mornings we would be given a hammer, a flatiron, and a bowl of nuts to crack and pick out for the homemade ice cream.

And there was the orchard beyond the kitchen window, the Wealthy, the Russet, the Wolf with its giant-sized fruit, and an apple romantically called the Northern Spy as if it were a suspicious character out of the Civil War.

All families had their special Christmas food. Ours was called Dutch Bread, made from a dough halfway between bread and cake, stuffed with citron and every sort of nut from the farm—hazel, black walnut, hickory, butternut. A little round one was always baked for me in a Clabber Girl baking soda can, and my last act on Christmas Eve was to put it by the tree so that Santa Claus would find it and have a snack—

after all, he'd come a long, cold way to our house. And every Christmas morning he would have eaten it. My aunt made the same Dutch Bread and we smeared over it the same butter she had been churning from their own Jersey (highest butter-fat content) cream that same morning.

To eat in the same room where food is cooked—that is the way to thank the Lord for His abundance. The long table, with its different levels where additions had been made for the small fry, ran the length of the kitchen. The air was heavy with odors not only of food on plates but of the act of cooking itself, along with the metallic smell of heated iron from the hard-working Smoke Eater, and the whole stove offered us its yet uneaten prospects of more goose and untouched pies. To see the giblet gravy made and poured into a gravy boat, which had painted on its sides winter scenes of boys sliding and deer bounding over snow, is the surest way to overeat its swimming richness.

The warning for Christmas dinner was always an order to go to the milkhouse for cream, where we skimmed from the cooling pans of fresh milk the cream which had the same golden color as the flanks of the Jersey cows which had given it. The last deed before eating was grinding the coffee beans in the little mill, adding that exotic odor to the more native ones of goose and spiced pumpkin pie. Then all would sit at the table and my uncle would ask the grace, sometimes in German, but later, for the benefit of us ignorant children, in English:

Come, Lord Jesus, be our guest,
Share this food that you have blessed.

There are no blessings like that any more: every scrap of food for which my uncle had asked the blessing was the result of his own hard work. What he took to the Lord for Him to make holy was the plain substance that an Iowa farm could produce in an average year with decent rainfall and proper plowing and manure.

The first act of dedication on such a Christmas was to the occasion which had begun it, thanks to the Child of a pastoral couple who no doubt knew a good deal about rainfall and grass and the fattening of animals. The second act of dedication was to the ceremony of eating. My aunt kept a turmoil of food circulating, and to refuse any of it was somehow to violate the elevated nature of the day. We were there not only to celebrate a fortunate event for mankind but also to recognize that suffering is the natural lot of men—and to consume the length and breadth of that meal was to suffer! But we all faced the ordeal with courage. Uncle Ben would let out his belt—a fancy western belt with steer heads and silver buckle—with a snap and a sigh. The women managed better by always getting up from the table and trotting to the kitchen sink or the Smoke Eater or outdoors for some item left in the cold. The men sat there grimly enduring the glory of their appetites.

After dinner, late in the afternoon, the women would make despairing gestures toward the dirty dishes and scoop up hot water from the reservoir at the side of the range. The men would go to the barn and look after the livestock. My older cousin would take his new .22 rifle and stalk out across the pasture with the remark, "I saw that fox just now looking for his Christmas goose." Or sleds would be dragged out and we would slide in a long snake, feet hooked into the sled behind, down the hill and across the westward sloping fields into the sunset. Bones would be thrown to dogs, suet tied in the oak trees for the juncos and winter-defying chickadees, a saucer of skimmed milk set out for the cats, daintily and disgustedly picking their padded feet through the snow, and crumbs scattered on a bird feeder where already the crimson cardinals would be dropping out of the sky like blood. Then back to the house for a final warming up before leaving.

There was usually a song around the tree before we were all bundled up, many thanks all around for gifts, the basket as loaded as when it came, more so, for leftover food had been piled in it. My father and uncle would have brought up the team from the barn and hooked them into the double shafts of the bobsled, and we would all go out into the freezing air of early evening.

On the way to the door I would walk under a photograph of my grandfather, his cavalry saber hung over it (I had once sneaked it down from the wall and in a burst of gallantry had killed a mouse with it behind the corncrib). With his long white beard he looked like one of the prophets in Hurlbut's illustrated *Story of the Bible,* and it was years before I discovered that as a young man he had not been off fighting the Philistines but the painted Sioux. It was hard to think of that gentle man, whose family had left Germany in protest over military service, swinging that deadly blade and yelling in a cavalry charge. But he had done just that, in some hard realization that sometimes the way to have peace and a quiet life on a modest farm was to go off and fight for them.

And now those bells again as the horses, impatient from their long standing in the barn, stamped and shook their harness, my father holding them back with a soft clucking in his throat and a hard pull on the reins. The smell of wood smoke flavoring the air in our noses, the cousins shivering with cold, "Good-by, good-by," called out from everyone, and the bobsled would slide off, creaking over the frost-brittle snow. All of us, my mother included, would dig down in the straw and pull the buffalo robes up to our chins. As the horses settled into a steady trot, the bells gently chiming in their rhythmical beat, we would fall half asleep, the hiss of the runners comforting. As we looked up at the night sky through half-closed eyelids, the constant bounce and swerve of the runners would seem to shake the little stars as if they would fall into our laps. But that one great star in the East never wavered. Nothing could shake it from the sky as we drifted home on Christmas.

The Holly

Green holly branch
With your red berry,
We hang you up
To make us merry.

Summer's colors
You keep bright,
Red and green,
In winter's white.

You are a sign
By night and day:
The time is good,
The house is gay.

A Handmade Christmas

That older Christmas was one we seemed to hold in our hands. After all, our hands seemed to create so much more of it then than now.

By needle, hammer, knife and saw we made the articles planned so long in advance. Mother always knew what all of us needed and was busy months ahead making shirts, coats, scarves, mittens, knitted caps, blouses, skirts, the multitude of clothes which a woman of average skill but of great determination and devotion could make on her own.

A few evenings before Christmas we would sit around big dishpans of popcorn, each child with a long thread and a needle, making strings of white corn to shine from branch to branch of the green tree. We had raised that corn ourselves in the garden behind the house. I had spent many hot mornings hoeing between the hills of corn, so that my feelings toward it were a little mixed. I always seemed to jab the kernels a lot harder than my sisters, so that the needle would break through and punch my skin. It was a miniature blood sacrifice, proper to that holiday which celebrated the birth, with its blood, of the God who would die in His blood.

There were also popcorn balls to be made just the size of baseballs, the sticky stuff shaped lovingly in our hands. The whole kitchen reeked of the crisp smell of corn and the sweet smell of hot syrup—and so did we. We would wrap oval, pointed butternuts in sheets of tinfoil, tying them with string so that they could be hung from the tree, to have a second and more glittering life back again in mid-air.

This was before tree stands had become so elaborate. My brother Bob and I would build a new frame out of boards every year, nailing together such a stout support as would outlast the needles themselves.

Of course, the greatest tree was the tall one at church on Christmas Eve, with its long candles wavering in the drafty air and a man standing at one side with a ten-foot pole which had a wet sponge tied on the end, ready to douse any fires that started. I fear that, along with the other children, we prayed as much for a really menacing fire to start as we did for the Christ Child.

There was always a church play on Christmas Eve, given at great cost to bed sheets and tempers. I was usually an anonymous shepherd with instructions to keep my grating voice low so as not to interfere with those who could sing. However, the shepherds carried crooks, which we used with deadly effect to trip the ankles of the splendid characters who had been the saintly Joseph and the Wise Men a few minutes before. The star that led the Wise Men across the desert traveled on a wire across the tiny stage, and often stuck halfway across, long before it reached the corner which was the barn where Joseph and Mary and the Child lay. One of the shepherds would then lift his crook to the starry heavens and shove that wayward star over where it belonged, sometimes bringing down the skies themselves.

After we had done the play, we were given our reward, a sack of candy from the tree, given out by a Santa Claus who looked and sounded remarkably like our fat barber and smelled like him, too, in an atmosphere of what was magically called "bay rum."

To my shame, one year I went back to the tree and,

pretending it was my first trip, received a second bag of candy. It sat untouched for days, as I wrestled with my conscience, which had been up to that crime a fairly feeble part of my life.

Finally I made a most human compromise. Torn between a sense of sin and my training never to waste anything, I managed to eat the stuff, but without enjoyment. It was ashes in the mouth, but at least it was not wasted.

Many of the gifts were made right in the family. My older brother usually had some wooden object out of his manual training class, a stool, a rack for the kitchen wall, while my sisters were busy with elaborately scrolled initials in the corners of handkerchiefs or with aprons on which whole gardens of flowers were appliquéd. I was too small to make anything except mischief, but my ambition was to whittle as well as my uncle on the farm, who could make a whistle which would really blow, carve little animals out of soft pine, or a tiny rifle with a peep-sight. Nevertheless, I tried and one year managed to chip and cut and beat a darning egg from a chunk of wood, sanding its awkward corners down, rubbing wax in until it was literally a handmade and hand-polished thing, wrapped in the fanciest paper I could find and presented to my mother as if it had been the Kohinoor diamond.

But was not Joseph, the father of Christ, a carpenter, and would he not have had a patient interest in a child's handwork out of wood?

It was our mother, of course, who made the most, something for every one of the four children, sewing late every night, hiding mysterious articles whenever one of us went through the little room off the kitchen where she had her sewing machine. By devotion, skill, and loss of sleep they would be finished and wrapped handsomely under the tree—the shirt, the coat, the dress—when we came down on Christmas morning.

Many years, going reluctantly to bed on Christmas Eve,

hanging over the stair railing for a last hope of seeing, if not Santa Claus himself, then at least a late-working mailman with a package, the last sound we heard would be that sewing machine. It was the old foot-powered Singer, whirring on into the late night on a final hem, resembling my mother in its strength for work, its steadiness, the cheerful sound it made. If I heard that treadle going tonight I would look across the room for a tree with candles and look out the window for a drift of snow like a great white candle sparkling. Most of all, I would want to hear it stop, to be followed by my mother's hurrying, bright steps going from sewing machine to Christmas tree with the last packages, weary but eager, the floor creaking as the house turned cold. That plain machine noise brings back our tears, our childhood, and our life.

It was also a mechanical noise that wakened us on Christmas morning, that angry but comforting sound which was my father shaking the cast-iron grates in our coal furnace. It was pleasant to burrow down in the covers knowing that in a few minutes, after that banging and shoveling had stopped, a little heat would creep timidly out of the hot-air registers. We had one register in the floor between two rooms and always hung a red paper bell over it, so that when the heat was really flowing up the bell would toss and sway in its silent ringing.

We made the paper cones that hung on the tree, and filled them with candy my sister Alice had boiled, poured and whipped in the kitchen. My reward for cracking the nuts we had gathered in gunny sacks after first frost on the farm (and for not eating all that I cracked) was scraping the pans. Somehow, the bits and dribblings I knocked loose tasted better than the beautiful neat squares on their trays. This did not keep me from stealing a few solid pieces when my sisters were not looking. Since the candy had been made for a solemn holiday, my beginning conscience would give me a bad time when I considered that I was actually at the start of a life of crime as a thief. This period of soul-searching usually lasted as long as it took my hand to lift up and snatch the candy. At that point I managed to beat down my spindly moral sense and to beat a fast retreat to another room, where I could contemplate my wickedness while eating the spoils.

The Bible has many references to caves, places where prophets lived, where Christ was taken after the Crucifixion. We had our own cave right in the house, a little closet with a miniature door. We could use it for play most of the year, hiding in it and scaring ourselves by closing the door and sitting in the dreadful dark. Weeks before Christmas, however, we had strict orders never to enter that closet, as it was my mother's hiding place for gifts. We would walk by, knowing that a quick pull on the door would reveal all the forbidden treasure, but somehow we realized the hallowed nature of the place, and not one of us ever looked. In the last few days before Christmas my mother would make many trips there with the presents she had made, and each trip made that odd place, which existed only because of a carpenter's error, a more secret and sacred cave.

It was a handmade Christmas. The entire family either sewed, whittled, knit, sawed, nailed, crocheted, embroidered, baked, pasted, or cracked to celebrate that generous Day with gifts. There was one object, however, which we made just for ourselves, the star for the top of the tree, cutting it from a stiff piece of cardboard. My job, as a zealous collector of leadfoil (like any one hundred per cent real American boy on his way to being President), was to produce some large sheets of the heavy stuff, not yet rolled into a ball to be sold by weight. This I did without revealing my sources of supply, as some of my brightest pieces smelled strongly of Horseshoe plug, and our Aunt Minnie considered nicotine an instrument of the devil.

We would wrap the star in my best leadfoil and tie it

on the highest point of the tree, where it could reflect the wavering wax candlelight, a handmade star, more wonderful to us than any in the sky because we had actually held it in our hands.

Not only was Christmas more personal then, it was also more exotic. We are all accustomed now to food and clothing brought to us from across America and from around the world, but when I was a child the things we ate and wore were much more local.

The tree itself, fir, pine, spruce (romantically called *evergreen*), was far outside the Iowa landscape, where elm, maple, oak lost their leaves each autumn as, it seemed to me, regular trees should. But these shipped in for Christmas were so strange it was as if they might have come from that far country where the birthday of the Child we were celebrating had taken place. It was exciting to look at the rows of evergreens suddenly appearing along the sidewalks in what is so expressively called the dead of winter. It was curious to go up and touch their hard shininess and smell their tang out of remote forests. In Iowa green was the color of pastures in June, of young corn, of new oats and hay, of living crops. Coming as they did in December, the Christmas trees brought a sense of the beginning of life, exactly at the time when our own landscape seemed to have no life in it at all.

What really brought the renewal of life to a child was the setting up of that tree in the house, its decorating, and then the magical moment when the true candles were lit and the whole green and romantic structure was covered with little, living flames. I was luckier then, in a wooden house in a small Iowa city, than the Child Himself, who had in all His childhood no such glittering thing to anticipate each year.

There were many other foreign-seeming objects in our Christmas. While I, like the man at church, sat by the tree with a wet sponge on a long rod, in case the tree caught fire from a candle (half hoping it would, and yet half fearful), all the children had a pile of exotic, once-a-year nuts. There were pecans, almonds and Brazil nuts, remarkable and unreal when compared to the hazel and hickory and butternuts from the farm. But most different of all was the "English" walnut. Our Iowa black walnut was a rugged thing, which stained our hands yellow-brown in gathering and had a shell so tough it had to be beaten with a hammer on a flatiron. These English walnuts, however, had fragile shells which my brother could crush in his hands, and meats which, while sweet, lacked the oily richness of our native black walnuts. It took brute strength to break through to the meat of our own kind, but the reward was a tastier and solider one.

We all hung our stockings from a table and every Christmas morning found in the toe a fresh orange, the only one we were sure of getting all year, for it was not a time when fruit traveled as gaily around the country as it does now. The orange, like the English walnut and the evergreen tree itself, came to our hands with a sense of distance about it. Surely that feeling is gone for children now, when they see oranges all the year round and weary of being told to drink their juice. We savored our orange section by slow section, and rubbed the aromatic skin on our noses, and felt in its orange-colored sweetness something of the far-off country of Palestine, a place famous for its oranges.

Although wiser heads have assured me that the orange may have come from Florida, the walnut from California, and the pine tree from Minnesota, and although my geography has expanded to include other continents, if not other stars, when all these objects come together at Christmas I still have a child's shock of being very close to the original village of Bethlehem in the desert where the first instant of the Christian Era began.

Like all decent Iowans, we had cousins in California who sent us boxes with pictures of palm trees, clusters of raisins, Chinese baskets with dragons circling them so that they scorched their own tails with the fire from their mouths. These also gave an exotic flavor to the season. It enchanted me to discover that branches of our own family lived in places which might be, to judge by the articles we received, not far from Judea, the fruit-growing country where that celebrated birth occurred. In the confusion of my mind at five years old the vast Iowa picnic at Los Angeles (and the very name of the city itself) became associated with the holiday and gave me a sense of participating in a great ceremony thousands of miles away. Later I was disillusioned, but for some years it gave me a powerful satisfaction to think that, through my cousins, I shared in that place and that event.

Perhaps the most exotic, and certainly the most exciting, object to come from far away was the annual huge box of candy from my Uncle George, who had gone west as a young man and set up a candy store near the Blackfoot Indian reservation in Idaho. He always included in his package a box of chocolates labeled "fancy," hand-dipped, with a "gold" spoon tied to the top by an orchid ribbon. The cover bore a full-length portrait of a scantily clad beauty, bold enough to stand there almost naked, but shy enough to turn slightly away from us all too eager viewers. This caused a certain amount of soul-searching among the more pious members of the family, who nevertheless always managed to eat a good share of the chocolates. Aunt Minnie simply ignored the daring young girl and looked on the cover as a landscape, commenting on what a nice waterfall that was.

So we made our Christmas, partly with our hands, partly with strange-seeming things long since become familiar. We scattered thimble cookies under the tree for any Brownies who happened to be passing by that night. There must have been a lot of them on the move, because by morning the little cookies would all be gone. We went to bed knowing that we had made such gifts as each child could at his own age, knowing that the whir of the sewing machine meant that our mother was still sewing on her own last gifts, and knowing that in the morning there would be a shining star on the tip of the Christmas tree, because we had shaped it ourselves and hung it there, long years before these new times in which men are trying to hang their new metallic stars in space. Will they have such hope and joy in their clever machines as we had, creeping reluctantly off to bed, in our plain star, silvery with leadfoil and reeking richly of that tobacco which Aunt Minnie fought with barehanded gallantry? We knew that in the morning she would come by and say, "Your tree always has such a pretty star."

She stood there in a collar she had crocheted for herself,

and we said nothing, for in her deceived innocence she was a part of the simple goodness of the times. With our hands we had made a part of her Christmas, as we had made a part of our own.

One of the most moving and expressive words in the English language is "handle." That childhood Christmas we made with our hands; their touch was on the things we gave, the food we raised.

From handling every sort of fabric, from using too many needles too rapidly so that the skin was broken, from scrapping and cutting too much food, from being in water far too hot, from being in the outside cold walking long distances to shop or bringing wood in from the backyard, Mother's hands would be, by the time Christmas Eve came, rough and hard and sore. But they were her live gift to Christmas: her working hands.

The hands of Christ's mother were probably such honest, working hands, as she lay in that chilly barn and handled the warm Child.

The Wreath

Now Christmas comes
Leafy and floral,
Poinsettia, pine,
The mountain laurel.

Now wreaths of fir,
Of spruce or pine
Hang on the door
With a green shine.

Even the sun,
On earth beneath,
Turns in space
Like a gold wreath.

And men who give
Love and good will,
Are a live wreath
On town and hill.

The Woman's Holiday

The Fourth of July was a man's holiday, loud, defiant, full of risk and explosion. The music was brass bands, martial and blaring. As some men were shooting off miniature cannon with a metallic roar, other men were hanging onto terrified horses; I remember the animals whinnying in fright and the men yelling at them in rage. The women did little to get ready for the Fourth, except pray that it would end rapidly and safely.

Christmas was a woman's holiday, quiet, sharing, full of cheer and generosity. The music was bright carols, which seemed to glow out of the singing mouths. As some women were stitching on skirts or crocheting odd, useless things, others were baking in the kitchen; I remember the wood-burning range, its fire humming a lively tune like a primitive carol which had warmed early Christians hiding out in their caves. As the kettles bubbled and the oven temperature rose higher, the air of that kitchen turned as crisp, flaky, and sweet-smelling as fresh bread.

Women began to get ready for Christmas many months in advance. In mother's case, our Christmas always began on the day after Christmas, when she would take me downtown to a store and open her "Christmas Club" for the next year. Her weekly contribution might be only a quarter or a half dollar, but it was her first concern and she would squeeze it out of the little she spent on groceries if need be. Of course, that club was a great thing in my life, for it meant that every week in the year we were reminded of the season of sharing. In the sultry August heat of our Iowa "dog days" we would go down and make our little celebration of the seriousness with which we believed in the holiday to come with the snow and the freezing winds out of the high western plains.

What brought the Holy Family to Bethlehem was a money matter; Joseph had to pay taxes in the town assigned to his tribe. The trip had to be made, and in winter, whether his wife was about to have a child or not. So it was that our tiny money affair of the club brought us into touch with the anticipation of Christmas; winter or summer, mother had to make that trip and pay her own little money offering. It was the happiest thing she did every week.

Why should Christmas not have been the most womanly of all celebrations? It was a day of praise for woman's most desirable and unique aspect: birth. In the dead season came life.

Feeling this appropriateness, women labored to make the day meaningful. In those days of few household appliances a woman with children and without any help put in a long, hard, laboring day. To that was then added all the extra Christmas thought and work. How did mother stand the grind of it? I can only assume that, to a sturdy farm upbringing, there was added a sturdy spirit uplifting.

Hands

God's glittering, wise hand
Laid the Christ Child on earth,
Giving Him in that barn
The pain and warmth of birth.

Out of that first great gift
That cried in the cold air
As if plain child, and not
Fragment of God were there,

Comes the good day when all
Across the living lands
Men, women, children touch
Their giving, taking hands.

He gave us His own Son.
Thus our own Christmas living
Is our poor human way
Of praising His first giving.

Newsboy's Christmas

As a carrier boy who delivered newspapers to a hundred families along a route of two miles, I probably knew more about the progress of Christmas each year than anyone else. Ministers of the Gospel, businessmen, housewives, all had their individual efforts to make for the holiday, but I alone had the total view.

After school I walked to the Cedar Rapids *Gazette* to wait with the other boys in a large room in the basement. This was heated by the furnaces where lead cylinders from other editions were melted down.

There was usually time to kill, so I read the paper and noted the Christmas news and the advertisements for gifts. That way, I kept informed of all the events and activities which were coming.

Then we lined up and received the papers, and as I put my canvas bag over my left shoulder (so that the right arm would be free for throwing papers onto porches), the depressing increase in thickness and weight told me that the cheerful season was approaching.

By the week before Christmas my shoulder would be pulled down by the heaviness of all that wood pulp given over to the news and business of those last days. There were afternoons when I would stagger with the load if I had to walk through snow or over ice, until the first few dozen papers had been thrown with a fine holiday thud onto the porches.

The day after Christmas the papers would be so thin that the bag would seem to have no weight at all. That lightness meant another year to wait.

Trudging across the business district to the beginning of my route, I passed the big store windows, and could tell by the changes in them that the holiday was near, and what sort of things were offered each year. This also meant that I walked under the street decorations which the city put up, so that I began my long hike by passing under arches of colored lights and pine boughs. *That* is the way for a boy to start out on his little job every day!

My route itself was a clear indication of the Christmas excitement. On some day two or three weeks ahead I would look up the long street where I began my delivery of the world's glories and disasters. Streets were not as brightly illuminated in those days, so that any new radiance would stand out conspicuously. And there, shining out of a window onto the reflecting snow, the light wavering because it came from flickering candles and not electric bulbs, would be the first Christmas tree of the year. It shone there like a star which came to rest on Earth instead of moving through the restless sky.

St. Matthew says: "And lo, the star, which they saw in the east, went before them, till it came and stood over where the young child was. When they saw the star, they rejoiced with exceeding great joy."

When I saw that tree, I rejoiced with exceeding great joy, for I knew the Day above all other days was close at hand. My bag of papers seemed lighter, and I knew that each time I walked up that street, laid out in the unique American manner, a mile straight before it curved, there would be more trees shining out into the cold, gay air.

By Christmas Eve, there was hardly a house in which I could not see the pine or spruce or fir bright in a room, and as I carried that same route for several years, I came to know which houses were first to put up a tree, which always had a huge one from floor to ceiling, and which had a tiny one on a table.

There was another thing I came to know along that length of houses: the people who lived there. I knew which houses had old men who dug around the yard in May, and would give me cuttings of roses and wax begonias to put in my bag and take home to start in our own yard.

More than that, I knew which houses had people who always gave the boy a token on Christmas Eve.

There were families which had their tree in a room shut off from the rest of the house until Christmas morning, and there were a few which, sadly, never put up a tree at all. But no matter what they did in advance of the Day, I distinguished the houses quite selfishly in terms of those which always had a gift for me, and those which did not.

One thing I discovered—the houses which began decorating early, with a wreath at door and window and a tree large and gaily hung with ornaments, were most likely to remember the paper boy.

For days ahead I began warming up my customers by making certain they thought of me. I would throw the paper up against the door with a brisk bang. This became easier to do as the editions became heavier, so that close to Christmas my route became a succession of formidable thuds as the thick papers struck door and porch.

Toward the end of the route, which went up to the last houses at the edge of the city, people would hear the paper and invite me in to get warm. My oldest customers knew that I had a long walk home, and understood that the trudge out from the center of town to the edge would chill any boy.

In somewhat the same way that hoboes are supposed to mark houses where they will get a generous reception, I had a precise knowledge of the places where I could expect a Christmas gift, all of the way out Fourth Avenue Southeast, to the city limits.

There was the last survivor of the Charge of the Light Brigade, a venerable Englishman who in summer gave me roses from plants he had brought from England. It was hard to imagine him as a young trooper riding into immortality on a fine bay horse, this quiet man digging in the black dirt which was such a wonder to him. But he had the saber and insignia to prove it.

He would wait for me on Christmas Eve, and I had orders to stop and knock. Inside, he would give me a fruitcake smelling richly of wine, and a half-dollar inside it. Standing there erect but gentle, and homesick for the green shire he would never see again, he would say, "Here, boy, real English cake, good for you in the winter."

The gifts would start quite close to the beginning of the route, so that as I went along throwing papers up to the doors, my bag would empty of the solid newspapers but I would replace them with little packages of gifts.

It was a comfort to me that the first gifts of all which I received were not from my own family, but from the people whom I was paid to serve. I was careful in throwing the paper on the porch on warm evenings not to hit the baby playing in its pen, to break no windows, not to leave the paper on the roof or under bushes.

They were glad to have me bring the daily record of what seemed worth praise or fear or shame or anger in the country and in the world. And I was glad to have a modest recognition once a year of their kind thought of me. It was a cheerful relationship, and gave me a much more sympathetic view of life than later years would allow.

An ironic and skeptical attitude toward experience is often right and fine, but there is a wisdom in kindness, too. I was lucky to discover that young, carrying newspapers on Christmas Eve.

The Glory of the Lord

The glory of the Lord
On Bethlehem was laid.
Men saw that radiant light
And they were sore afraid.

An angel said, Fear not,
Tidings of great joy
I bring you. In a barn
Is born a holy Boy.

Now by His shining face,
And by His living voice,
The turning earth will glow.
Look at it and rejoice.

Forever now, when plain
Daylight warms this place,
The whole round world will glow,
Radiant as His face.

Christmas Means Family

ne December 23 I spent the day at Kennedy International Airport in a snowstorm. The runways were nearly all blocked with snow, but now and then a plane would leave. It was this occasional sound of engines which kept many thousands of half-hopeful people there, because that sound meant one plain and yet magical word—*home,* to the family.

Over and over, as I walked past little groups sitting with their luggage, or standing at the windows staring forlornly out the windows at the swirling menace, I overheard the same phrase—"home with the family by Christmas." It was all the hope for all of us. The mere chance of reaching their families in every far corner of the USA in time for the great holiday at the end of the year, kept restless crowds of weary people waiting in discomfort many hours. And yet, unlike other crowds I have been with at airports when weather imposed delays, this was a patient and cheerful crowd, for the hope of home and family kept them so.

This is only true of Christmas. We do not try desperately to rush home for the Fourth of July. Only Christmas has this live power of family attraction. This is as it should be, for the original event on a cold desert night of conspicuous stars was a family affair. Indeed, what could be more like our own day than the reason for Joseph and Mary making that trip in an uncomfortable season—they had gone to pay their taxes. Childbirth and taxes—are these not our own life also?

Christmas was always a close family matter for us. It began months before, and was no matter of hasty shopping for some slick present a few days earlier. Our children, two daughters, always made by hand several presents for their parents and for each other. One year Mary, then five, made a doll for Sara, then one. Friends in for Christmas Eve were a little startled to hear Mary, when I told her it was time for bed, reply firmly, "But I can't go now. I have to stuff a leg."

Mary slashed off a hank of her own hair before we knew it, and stitched it onto the doll's head, so that part of her was forever a part of it. The doll was taken to bed every night by Sara, and was clutched by her for comfort in the long, dark hours. Mary's left hand was in Christmas colors that day. Holding the doll as the unskilled fingers of her right hand worked the needle, she pricked the skin several times. The red blood was covered with a green bandage, to her great pride.

Of course, all planning of gifts for small children has to be done without illusions about the unpredictable choices they will make. One year we had found a wonderful wooden train of gaily painted cars on wheels which could be pulled in a curving line over the floor. The cars were unpacked, each held up eagerly, and the whole train hooked together, pulled once around the room, and left. A few minutes later Sara came in dragging by an old string a line of wooden blocks and cakes of soap which she had laboriously put together herself months before. All day she pulled this homemade thing while the gleaming gift sat in a corner; naturally, she preferred the cherished and familiar object to the bought toy. Her own life was mixed with it.

Sara also made gifts as soon as she could use her hands. They were largely for the animals which she acquired in as large quantities as we would allow. (With some animals, alas, acquiring one was only the first innocent step to the astonishment of coming down one morning and finding five small new ones.) Her first effort was a winter blanket for a tiny Chihuahua dog. The stitches were far apart, the blanket hung down on one side so far the poor dog tripped on it, but it actually had a crude fastener in front and the pooch became very attached to it. The cloth had been the tail on an ancient wool shirt of mine, so that I knew intimately just how warm it could be. The dog trotted proudly off through the snow in his uneven garment as if it had been tailored at Brooks Brothers. He also used it for sleeping on cold nights.

The whole family made things. The children's mother sewed beautifully, often making miniature clothes for the dolls which matched the dresses she had made for Mary and Sara. The girls were as happy, in fact, at receiving a box of little hats, shirts and blouses for their favorite dolls, as they were at receiving the same items for themselves. These were sensibly made with big snaps which the small fingers could really work. The dolls were always carefully prepared on Christmas Eve, just as if they were live children, properly dressed, then shown the lights on the Christmas Tree, carried around the neighborhood to view other trees, outdoors or seen through windows. Then they were undressed and put to bed with warnings not to peek before morning. In this way, the girls doubled their own pleasure by sharing it with their dolls. How dull Christmas next door seemed, where there were only boys, crashing around with hockey sticks and wind-up toy automobiles!

Mary received a "bake-with-mother" cooking set one Christmas, from our friends Owen and Leone Elliott, and in the following years, being an instinctively domestic child, she

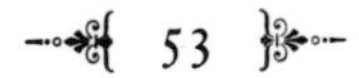

always prepared her own tiny cookies, the sort which my own sisters a long time before had called "thimble cookies." We had some old-fashioned houses of heavy paper, assembled to make a little village under the tree. Mary would always refer to these as the Brownie houses, and leave a pile of her cookies by each one for the nourishing of whatever Brownies had been out all night stuffing children's stockings with gifts, obviously an exhausting and hunger-making job.

One Christmas I found a second-hand wicker doll carriage, battered but sturdy. I painted it in a neighbor's garage. My wife sewed a perfectly-fitting pad, some small blankets, and even made from some wool a "snuggle-bunny" which would hold a doll. On Christmas morning I brought it over, where it was radiantly accepted as the one gift which could contain everything the girls most loved. First they put all of their dolls in, wheeling them rapidly around the room, and then shoving it back and forth between them. Later I found Mary pushing Sara in it, the smaller child fitting exactly into the doll carriage. (This sisterly devotion went on until Sara's legs had grown so long her feet hung down over the front of the carriage.) Mary was very proud to wheel her live doll down the street with neighborhood friends who had only ordinary dolls. Of course, she would sometimes run with the sleeping girl bouncing over the rough spots, turning corners on two wheels.

Sara took over the carriage when she was older and would put her two tiny dogs in it, tucking them under the blankets with only their wrinkling noses and uneasy eyes peering out. She said her dolls didn't scratch afterward, no matter what jokes Mary made about that.

One of the great Christmases happened the year I brought home a used hobby-horse. It was a beautiful animal, with a miniature saddle and bridle, strong enough for Sara to get on and ride. This she did all day, putting the horse into mad gallops which sometimes went so fast the frame on which the horse was suspended would lift from the rug. There was one sad lack—the tail had been lost. We agreed with Sara that it disfigured the lovely creature, so I went to a friend who had horses and persuaded him to cut some from one of his animals which was the proper color.

It was winter, the horse had been rolling in the barnyard, it had not been brushed. First the cleaning, so we put the mess into a pan of hot water along with soap powder. Soon the gay cinnamon scent of our Christmas baking faded from the air and in its place the whole house was permeated with the most revolting animal stench. Turning our too delicate city noses away from the pan, we sudsed that foul wad of hair. Then it had to be dried by a hot air register, which effectively stank up whatever far corners had escaped the odor of cooking horsehair. But by the end of Christmas Day the new horse had a long tail, holding it high with the help of some glue which Sara managed to spread over her hands and face. Sara took the hair which was left over and made herself a tail out of it, wearing it gaily behind her for years of cantering from room to room with a fine whinny.

We always made strings of fresh white popcorn to scatter through the green tree like ropes of snow. There was Indian corn of many colors, and we could string that if we got it soft, before the kernels hardened and became too flinty for a needle in the hands of children. Many of the ornaments would be homemade, too—paper horns of candy and walnuts wrapped with gold and silver paper, tiny figures of angels Mary sewed together from scraps of white silk, and figures of old-fashioned girls she made from lovely fragments found in a trunk. The latter had elegant underwear made from lace taken from a grandmother's corset cover. We were not quite certain that it was proper to have the angel looking across at the froth of fancy slip peeking out from under the skirts, but always put them back on the tree in the slippery belief that sin was not in so shy an action, and that if it was anywhere, it would be in the mind of the beholder.

There was the exotic year when Mary found a box of scallop shells gathered on eastern Long Island along Gardiners Bay the summer before. She took crayons and drew many miniature pictures of shore birds, beach plants, gulls and sandpipers, cranberries found red and shiny in the dunes. These were put inside the shells, holes punched with an ice pick through shell and picture, all then tied together with gaily colored yarn to make actual books. Some she gave to us and others she hung on the tree, so that, among the midwestern decorations we had made, and the handsome ornaments my family had brought from the Black Forest three generations before (how did they stand the rough journey to a seaport, the stormy passage in a frail sailing vessel, the trip by train and oxcart out to frontier Iowa? but how did the mother of Christ stand the jolting trip by donkey to Bethlehem?), we had these cheerful reminders of the sea. The gravest danger to ornament, doll figure and shell book was, of course, the childish fingers handling them, and yet not one was broken. Such is the true spirit of Christmas—it can give sense and caution to the most exuberant fingers.

My most selfish Christmas arrived with a heavy, square box under the tree. Opening it, I found a new portable typewriter, which I terribly needed. My wife had earned it by designing and making and selling thousands of original Christmas cards. It was a gift which came out of strained eyes and hands knicked on the sharp edges of cut paper. I wrote six books on it.

My most embarrassing Christmas came when I bought my wife one of those elaborate dress forms which could be cunningly adjusted to reproduce any woman's figure. It was stored with a friend a few houses away, fully expanded in all its majestic lines. I carried it back in my arms in deep snow on Christmas Eve. Surely this is the most awkwardly shaped article any man could pick up in his arms. I stumbled through ruts and slipped on ice, clutching what must have seemed to my admiring neighbors some strange blonde I was trying to sneak into the house. You can't disguise a dress form; it just looks like itself, when seen close up, so my gift was identified the instant I entered the house, in spite of the sheet I had thrown over it and the red ribbon tied on its majestic bosom.

We always used Christmas, as my family had used it before, as a way of giving the children necessary clothing which we had let go until then. This resulted in some of the gifts being anticipated, although there was always some uncertainty about their exact characteristics. Mary, opening a box with a new sweater: "Oh mother, I thought you'd give me that blue one we looked at in the window. But this is the color I *really* wanted." Sara, taking out of vast wrappings a honey-colored pigskin saddle for her young horse: "That's just the size my mare needs, and I can always darken that icky color with neat's foot oil." And then she hugged it to her, the stirrup leathers hanging around her neck, as if it had been a longed-for doll.

Because Christmas had been this close family matter, it was natural, when we were talking about the possibility of getting a second car, somewhat as a holiday present to the whole family, Sara should say, "I think a one-ton truck would be nice. Then I could use it to haul my horses. Think of the kids I could drive to school." It is my guess that, if there is a car in one of our stockings hanging from the mantel some year soon, it will be a one-ton truck.

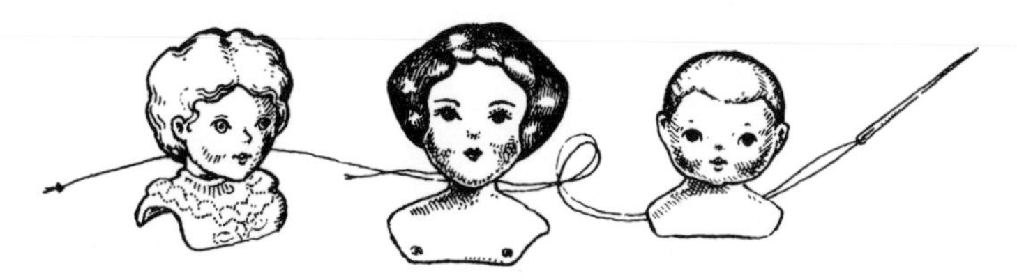

The Animals

Animals knew Him
In His first sleep,
Donkey and cow,
The wool-soft sheep.

The humblest beasts
Gave Him their heat,
And shared the straw
Beneath their feet.

Creatures were kind
In that cold place.
They gave Him warmth.
He gives us grace.

Come Home!

hristmas glitters with lights and glows with wreaths. The ornamented tree stands like a gesture of hope—a bush which we have set burning right in the corner of our room. The gifts make their own illumination of time spent and thought taken. The whole season is fiery with gay color and warm feeling and the perpetual smile of green in the gray winter.

Yet all of this luminous animation has one meaning rising and shining above all others. This is the simple but incandescent cry which men and women and children have uttered as a bright sound out of the darkness of time—Come home! Come home!

When the Wright brothers had finally made their flimsy plane lift itself by its own power from the sandy beach at Kitty Hawk, they sent a telegram.

After telling the success of their visionary effort to get man off the ground and into the sunlit air, they added the most touching two words they could have sent: "Home Christmas."

It is not only comforting, but exciting and, at the same time, perfectly natural, that two men should have done this. What is more a part of our heritage than to get home by Christmas? Having put a machine with a man just enough above the solid earth to suggest that they would soon be in the sky, the brothers at once thought of the annual celebration of that event which had been marked by the flight of a star in the sky.

It is warming to know that the result of flying was to make these marvelous inventors want to flee home and, with their family, observe that one holiday in our calendar which is devoted to the most marvelous invention in the history of human life: The presence of God in a newborn Child.

Christmas is the intense family celebration. Other holidays are for the church; are like Easter, for example, the great ceremony celebrated by ecstatic music and the rectangular agony of the Cross, observed in church with ritual. National days are honored with speeches, parades, the ceremonies of civil order. But Christmas, like birthdays, is glorified above all in the home, for it too is a birthday. It is the renewal of the great covenant of a man and woman having children on the living earth.

There is a pathetic irony in this holiday. The supreme birth is that of Christ, and it is His day which draws the Christians of the world home to celebrate it. Yet Christ was born away from home, on a journey which symbolized the restless and wandering nature of His whole life. The symbol of birth and security and home was born in the insecurity of a barn, with unaware animals. Yet this was right, too, for it was His destiny not to have a house, a family, a settled life, but to roam the roads and towns of Israel, and finally to die in the solitary ordeal of the Crucifixion, so that out of His loneliness all others should have the shared life of a home.

Even when Jesus was twelve years old, He stayed on in Jerusalem alone when His parents left for home. They did not miss their Child for a day, then returned, and only after three days of searching did they find Him, disputing in the temple with the priests. In an amusing assertion of family authority the Gospel of St. Luke says that when Christ went home with His mother and father, He "was subject unto them." Even God-on-earth accepted the control of His parents, although He had gone away from it four days.

Even after his birth in the rude discomfort of the barn, an angel of the Lord appeared to Joseph in a dream and said that he should arise and take the young Child and the mother and flee into Egypt, for Herod would slay all of the young children. Thus Christ, born on a journey, was not allowed the temporary home of an animal shelter, but had to go off on another journey into exile. He gave His life to save ours, and gave up His home to let us have a home.

The deepest search of human life is the constant and strenuous effort to find a place where one can be "at home." In this century, when the formidable threat of the mass may replace the close unit of the family with the massive unit of abstract society, the home has an intolerably greater importance. It was Christ's glorious and bloody destiny to find His home only in death. It is the fortunate and nourishing destiny of men and women to find an intimate home here on the harried earth.

Years before he walks *away* from the home in which he took his first faltering step over a floor that seemed waiting to leap up and strike him, the child learns that in the rooms of the place where he lives there are assurance and trust. At the level of his exploring eyes, there are the legs of chair and table, even of adults and older children, to which he can cling when miniature knees wobble. Above all, when he does reel and collapse with the indignity of bumps, bruises and tears, there is a hand to help and a voice to comfort. Toys are there on the floor of the home, too, bear and elephant, the pictured book and the squeaking box. The child life roams in the cheerful wilderness of household menace and love.

Gradually the child finds that there is an immense world beyond the reach of his hands or even his eyes. This world is in other rooms, the enchanting places of huge beds where adults sleep like a race of giants which has come to protect the real people (the children) and not to destroy them. Of course, now and then the adults do seem to threaten, but unaccountably, after the punishment for some troubled act has been given, and the child reduced to fright and wailing, always the devoted arms come and the child is wonderfully back in its own true home, the magical, narrow space between arm and breast.

There is that mysterious room where the nose and the tongue are excited, the kitchen. Here the child moves from having his hand slapped as he reaches to grasp a knife, to having his hand reached for and held a moment while the savory sweetness of a broken cookie is put in it. In this room, the child senses are alive, for it is the one room in the house where touch, taste, sight, sound, smell all are fulfilled. Most of all, Christmas heightens every awareness of the child, as home becomes filled with more light, more odors to tease the nose, more gifts for the eager hand to caress.

Then the child is old enough to venture outdoors, perhaps even down the street, where live other children, about whom only an uncertain curiosity exists. There may be dogs there, friendly with a head to be scratched or hostile with a head showing its tearing teeth. Always, when pursuing the brave adventure of the next city block, or the new stretch of country road, the child can look back and know that there is one fixed absolute waiting in assurance behind it—home. A pillar of cloud by day and of fire by night, home stands there; the child runs to it in terror or delight, pursued by angry children or outraged dogs, or only by the illusion of evil, seeming to sniff the ground where the child's feet had stepped.

This is the first homecoming, this flight from play, or from school, to the fortified place where all is certainty and trust. My own daughter came excitedly back from school one day when she was tiny. My wife and I were outside the house in the backyard and heard her first cheerful cry as she called out that she was home. When we made no reply, her voice called again, but now trembling. Her small shout echoed through the empty rooms and we heard her feet running in fright. Then she fled into the yard and saw us there. Pretending that she had not been frightened at all, she came slowly up and took my hand and said simply, "I'm here!" But she gave it all away, for as she spoke in mock bravery, one tear (dark because of the darkness of her desolation at finding us not where she hoped), fell on my hand, and stung with its emotional salt. Here is the poem which I wrote about that homecoming. It is from my book *American Child,* a sequence of one hundred sonnets on the myriad ways in which a daughter discovers the terrifying but irresistible world:

I'm home! I'm home! I'm home!
Runs in and bangs the door,
Throws down her book and comb,
Coat, mittens, on the floor.
Waits doubtfully, then calls
Again, fearing her fear,
When the room's empty walls
Cry, No one! No one here!

Then turns and runs outside,
Finding us waiting there,
And says in her small pride,
Clutching my hand with care,
And dropping one dark tear,
I'm here! I'm here! I'm here!

In a few years, the child is only part a child, and has gone out into the semi-exile of the adult world, where strangers prowl the uneasy streets and glare from the windows with their sinister curtains. Here the child discovers one of the vast and shattering truths about human life—that these other people, far from being themselves hard and secure, are like the new one who comes to move among them. They, too, are still in part children, making their successes and failures, their whole lives and their half-lives, but always a little homesick for the plain room of their childhood, in whose air hung the most glittering ornament of all, the knowledge that a cry would bring comfort. From this he gains disillusion, for he now knows that wherever his life may take him, no fine triumph, and no harsh defeat, will ever remove from his mind the awareness of that original place where he learned to become alive.

The satellites glide overhead, glow through the sky like rapid, tiny moons. But the most startling illumination in our lives will always be the lighted window, behind which we know (and we know it with a desperate, earned conviction) there waits the parent, who now, having yearned for the infrequent letter or the remote telephone call, now endures the final minutes before we open that door and go into the room, into the love, into *home.* No other door of our lives ever opens into such a confidence of outgoing acceptance and enfolding arms.

By now the child has become himself a parent, and has made his other startling discovery—he has now become the creator himself of that lamp-lit space, a room in which a child tries out his voice and hands, and totters on untrustworthy legs toward the trusted arms, which turn out to be his own. He now possesses two places, possesses them emotionally, as one does not possess property—the home of his childhood, and the home where he sees the new child moving almost as strangely as a creature from outer space.

So, at Christmas, he decorates the tree and instructs the child in anticipation and giving. He knows that, when the first restless man puts his human foot on the indifferent moon, he will test the density not only of the atmosphere but of his continuing concern for the child back on earth, testing the breathed air of room and yard and street. For he will know that there are two enchanting lights which the human eye cannot resist. One is the glow of the remotest star whose rays flicker with the traversing of fantastic distance and overwhelming light years. Is there life out there, a life of child and house?

The other light which moves us to an equally strong speculation is the steady and ardent glow in a child's eye, reflecting the room's lamp, or the love in our own eye, or the incandescence of the Christmas tree, which lights all of us home in the dark month of the year.

The Lamb

While shepherds watched
Their flocks that night,
Sheep watched their lambs
In that cold night.

While not far off
With human care
The Lamb of God
First breathed live air.

Now Christ the Lamb
Of plain barn-birth,
Shepherds men on
The human earth.

The Origin of Christmas

nly one event in the world's unbelievable history really divides time. That is the birth of a Child on a cold night in sandy country. We call it Christmas. Everything which has happened to mankind is dated before or after that event.

There was opposition at first to observing the birthday of Christ. Origen in the third century said that it should not be celebrated "as if He were a Pharaoh." But the celebration of so touching and crucial a birth was irresistible. By A.D. 388 St. John Chrysostom was writing that the Feast of the Nativity was not quite ten years old.

Although the pagan world had devised ceremonies and legends connected with the winter solstice, lighting fires and hanging up green to persuade the sun to bring its warmth back, the birth of Christ had qualities about it which no previous rituals had conceived. There was a gentleness which was new. One of the stories relates that the ox in the stable at Bethlehem was so moved by the holy presences that he was afraid to draw breath for fear of breathing in an angel.

When halos appeared above the heads of Joseph, Mary and the Child, the ox said that he and the ass must be too insignificant to deserve one. The ass amusingly replied he, at least, had carried the Virgin. There was such a radiance in the air that the ox felt it in the water, and would not drink any substance which had known the luminous air around the Child. So he went over to some muddy water and drank that; yet even he felt an infinite sweetness in the throat.

An act which could attract such stories obviously had to be celebrated. The persecuted Christians in the catacombs under Rome drew pictures on the walls showing the Adoration of the Magi. The observance of a life-creating event brought a renewal of life to the participants. It was said that on the first Christmas, trees bloomed which never bore flowers in winter. In Alsace it was said that a rose bloomed not in its season but on Christmas, for it was from the stock on which Mary hung her Baby's swaddling clothes on the flight into Egypt.

It was in the tomb of Joseph of Arimathea that Jesus was laid. The legend says that Joseph came to England (bringing the Holy Grail), planted his staff, and died. The staff grew to a thorn tree, from which slips were planted in the neighborhood. They always bloomed at Christmas.

The great pagan festivals celebrating the winter solstice took place in December. Sun worship was a profound part of these early religions, so that it must not have been chance that the birthday of Christ was established by the Church Fathers in a month which was traditionally devoted to the worship of new life.

In Rome, the festival of Saturn was held in December. It was accompanied by unrestrained merrymaking, extending even to the slaves. The orgies which occurred then later gave the name Saturnalia to any extreme revelries.

In northern Europe there were December festivals in honor of a god of golden sunshine, with dances, feasting, and religious rites. In Scandinavia it was called the time of Yule.

When Saint Augustine was sent by Pope Gregory in A.D. 579 to convert the people of England, he was told to study the native practices of the people, and where they were not vicious, to adapt them to Christianity. This shrewd decision resulted in the survival to this day of many Christmas observances which might otherwise have been destroyed as being too pagan.

It is likely that the Christmas tree came from the worship of oak and mistletoe by the Druids. The Druidic priests, wearing white ceremonial robes, went into the forests of oak where mistletoe grew on the branches and cut it down with a golden sickle. It would be taken to an altar and burned in sacrifice. The mistletoe was considered a symbol of hope and peace and good will. Under the mistletoe, even old enemies dropped their weapons and embraced. Thus the custom of kissing under the mistletoe descended from this ancient rite.

The yule log seems to have continued the bonfires lit as part of the sun worship rituals. It was St. Boniface in the eighth century who replaced the pagan oak, used for primitive ceremonies, with the fir tree, bearing candles, to celebrate the Christ Child.

There is a story that the crèche began with St. Francis. In his intense enthusiasm for making Christmas resemble the first scene as closely as possible, St. Francis made a manger in a village church. He filled the chancel with hay and led an ox and an ass down the aisle. He had a mother sit with her young baby alongside the animals. The clergy said that he was crazy, but the villagers loved it.

In Germany there is an account of a forester's hut in a storm on Christmas Eve. A knock was heard at the door, and an exhausted child entered. Little Hans gave the stranger his bed. In the morning the family was wakened by the singing of choirs of angels and the little guest was transfigured. It was the Christ Child, who broke a branch from a fir tree and set it in the earth, saying, "This is my gift to you. This tree shall always bear its fruit at Christmas."

In the lower Rhineland clogs of wood were put out by children for Santeklas, or St. Nicholas, along with hay for his horse. St. Nicholas once gave three bags of gold to a merchant who could not marry off his daughters because they had no dowry. Hence the three golden balls of the pawnbroker's sign as symbols of the protection St. Nicholas gave to merchants.

In medieval times the legend of Adam and Eve was celebrated by a procession in the streets. Adam carried the tree of life hung with apples. The green tree defied winter devils, and burning juniper was used to chase away demons. A tree would be hung upside down from the ceiling and decorated.

In France as in other countries the Yule log was always ignited by a piece from the previous year's log, and wine was spilled on it as a blessing. Grain would be planted in little dishes on December 4; if it sprouted abundantly by Christmas, the crops would be good. Sheaves of wheat would be tied up on the house. The children would build the Christ Child's crèche from stones, branches, moss and lichens. The cat would be given all it could eat, for if it mewed on Christmas Day it was bad luck. The Day was called Noel because it brought good news (*nouvelles*).

From the eleventh to the seventeenth centuries in England, the days from Christmas Eve to Twelfth Night were celebrated with gaiety which came close to debauchery. There were a Lord of Misrule and a Jester, mummers, masques, humor which at times became rough. In 1644, at the Long Parliament, the Puritans abolished Christmas. This stern attitude carried over into New England, where laws were passed making work on Christmas Day compulsory. Indeed, a man could be jailed for *not* working on Christmas. After all, the day of Christ's birth had not been honored in the Old Testament.

In England Christmas was a time of continual conviviality. Amateur players called "mummers" (from the masks they wore) went around doing entertainments and little plays in the streets. They were full of such cheerful greetings as:

A merry Christmas and a happy new year,
Your pockets full of money and
your cellar full of beer.

In Coventry an actor in a play who represented God in "The Creation" received three shillings, fourpence; Judas, properly enough, received only fourpence, but was paid another fourpence for crowing like a rooster, the first time that Judas also made the noise announcing his own betrayal.

These plays began to have too much violence and broad humor and were prohibited for a time. Indeed, in Puritan

England ministers were forbidden to preach God's word on the Nativity. In 1647 the parish officers of Westminster were fined and imprisoned for allowing preaching on Christmas Day and for decorating the church with rosemary. The famous diarist Evelyn and his family were arrested for taking the sacrament on Christmas. On December 24, 1652, Parliament ordered that "No observance shall be had of the five and twentieth day of December, commonly called Christmas Day; nor any solemnity used or exercised in churches."

The old days in England were often so excessive in their celebrations that one can imagine a reaction to them. When Richard II held Christmas at Litchfield, 2,000 oxen and 200 tuns of wine were consumed. Here is a suggested menu for a moderate Christmas dinner: Sixteen dishes in all, "a shield of brawn with mustard; a boyl'd capon; a boyl'd piece of beef; a chine of beef, rosted; a neat's tongue, rosted; a pig, rosted; chewets, baked; a goose, rosted; a swan, rosted; a turkey, rosted; a haunch of venison, rosted; a pasty of venison; a kid, with a pudding in the belly; an olive-pye; a couple of capons; a custard." To these were added "sallets, fricases, quelques chose" to make the entire service thirty-two dishes.

Brawn was a pickled and jellied loaf made from the head and feet of a boar, with occasionally ears thrown in. When the French army took Calais from the English, a great quantity of brawn was found. The French roasted, oiled and baked it, but found it inedible. Then someone simply ate a piece as it was and found it tasty. Monks tasted it, and said it was fish and could be eaten on fast days.

Boar's head was a ceremony at Christmas dinner, and often peacock was served, sometimes with the head and beautiful tail feathers of the bird sticking out above the dish. At court there was often gay sport, including tumbling.

Often the gifts which tenants were to give their landlords were written out in the lease, a pathetic distortion of real Christmas spirit. But gifts could be as simple as a goose, or as elaborate as Sir Francis Drake's 1589 present to Queen Elizabeth: "A fan of white and red feathers, the handle of gold, enameled with a half-moon of mother of pearl, within that a half-moon garnished with sparks of diamonds, and a few seed pearls on one side, having her majesty's picture within it, and on the other side a device with a crow over it."

But the real Christmas was not (is not) the merely gay, the dinners with "pies of carps' tongues," the Elizabethan masque called "Love freed from Ignorance and Folly." It was (and is) the coming of the first Christmas tree to Windsor Castle, introduced by the German Prince Consort, Albert, to Queen Victoria in 1841, the spontaneous giving which survives all commercial zeal, the profound renewal of faith in life, which is faith in God, by the contemplation of a Child whose first breath was shared with animals. It was the taking over of the ancient use of holly and making it a Christmas symbol, for Mary's Child had a crown of thorns and drops of red.

Christmas is Dr. Albert Schweitzer bringing in a tiny tree to a hopelessly ill patient in his African hospital, lighting the candles, and singing carols with the voice which had spoken the dread diagnosis to the stranger. It is President Harrison being Santa Claus in the White House. It is the old English song:

Heap on more wood—the wind is chill;
But let it whistle as it will,
We'll keep our Christmas merry still.

The Lights

As once in that
Old desert sky
Was hung the star
Men traveled by,

So on cold earth
In this year, we
Hang the warm lights
On our tall tree.

Now in the month
Of long, dark nights,
We put out strings
Of long, gay lights,

That men may know
Hope still can glow
On earth below
Through night and snow.

Early American Christmas

The Pilgrims who landed at Plymouth (first called Thievish Harbor because an Indian had stolen a harpoon there) in 1620 celebrated their first Christmas in the manner which they felt proper —by working hard and refusing to acknowledge that it was the Day of Nativity.

They were still living on the Mayflower and going ashore to build "ye first house for comone use." The Pilgrims considered as a "human invention" the idea of Christmas, for which there was no warrant in Scripture. They viewed it as a pagan survival, and argued that no one could be a true Christian who observed December 25 as a holiday.

The records of the colony declare "no man rested all that day." Back at the ship, they were distressed to find that their victuals were "much spente, especially our Beere," and they were reduced to drinking water.

But the skipper of the Mayflower, an Englishman who was not a Pilgrim, and believed in the traditional cheerful ways of observing Christmas, broke out a barrel of the ship's beer and invited the Pilgrims to share it, which they did most gladly. The men left on shore had no beer and complained bitterly.

The second Christmas in the New World was darkened for the Pilgrims by an Indian scare. They decided to build, at great labor for the few men there, a palisade, eleven feet high and a mile in circumference around their houses.

On Christmas morning they prepared to go out and work on it as usual, but many of the men who were not Pilgrims "excused themselves and said it wente againste their consciences to work on that day." Governor Bradford said that he would excuse them if it were a matter of conscience.

But when Bradford came back at noon with those who had been working, he found the non-Pilgrims not in their houses devoutly honoring Christmas, but "in ye street at play, openly; some pitching ye barr, & some at stooleball, and such like sports."

Bradford took away their implements of sport and told them that it was against his conscience that they should play while others worked. "If they made ye keeping of it a matter of devotion, let them keepe their houses, but there should be no gaming or reveling in ye streets."

From then on, no playing on Christmas.

At Boston, the Puritans believed that Christ's birth was too serious a matter to be celebrated by the fallen and sinful race He had come to save. It was wicked to be jolly on Christmas Day when you did not know if you would be damned to everlasting punishment. In 1659 a law was passed that, "Whosoever shall be found observing any such day as Christmas . . . either by forbearing of labour, feasting, or any other such way . . . shall be subjected to a fine of five shillings." (At the time, this is estimated at $7.)

The first Christmas observed in Boston was in 1686. The Puritans would not allow Governor Andros to use one of their churches for such a hellish purpose, so he had to use the Town House. Opposition to this was so strong that he had to go to the celebration with an armed guard on each side. Christmas was not a legal holiday in Boston until 1856.

At Salem in 1705 Samuel Sewall was indignant that the Anglicans celebrated Christmas on Saturday and then on Sunday went to the harbor "Rummaging and Chittering with Wheelbarrows & to get aboard at the Long Wharf, and Firing Guns and Setting Sail." For Sewall, as for all pious Massachusetts men, Sunday was the proper day for worship, not Christmas.

The great New England preacher, Cotton Mather, whose sermons were delivered with such warmth that the worshippers could smell the sulphurous odor of hellfire in them, protested in 1711: "I hear a Number of people of both Sexes, belonging many of them to my Flock, have had on the Christmas night, this last week, a Frolick, a revelling Feast, and a Ball, which discovers their corruption, and has

a Tendency to corrupt them yett more, and provoke the Holy One to give them up into eternal Hardness of Heart." Mather raged against Christmas, saying that it was an affront to the grace of God for men to use the birth of the Saviour by "mirth, by long eating." This latter certainly eliminated my family.

When King's Chapel at Boston, the Church of England edifice, burned in 1753, the congregation could find no suitable place to have a Christmas service. Although the Puritans still believed that it was wrong to attend church on Christmas, the feeling had become a little less rigid, and the Old South congregation voted to allow their Episcopalian friends to hold services in their meeting house, provided that it was not decorated with spruce or greens.

The famous Captain John Smith sailed for America in 1606, but the winds were unfavorable and Christmas was spent in sight of England, with many sick. "We made the best cheer we could," he says.

The next Christmas, having founded Jamestown in Virginia, Smith was a captive of the Indians, but was saved, as every school child knows. On a later Christmas, Smith wrote: "The extreme winde, rayne, frost and snow caused us to keep Christmas among the salvages where we weere never more merry, nor fed on more plenty of good Oysters, Fish, Flesh, Wild Fowl and good bread, nor ever had better fires in England."

The Dutch who settled Manhattan Island in the seventeenth century brought over their gay customs. The ship in which they came had St. Nicholas as a figurehead. It was declared that from December 14 to three weeks after Christmas there should be no meetings of the Council, which presumably would be too busy (1654) celebrating to bother with governing.

Washington Irving recorded the Dutch dinner with pious enthusiasm and witty delight. "There was the doughty doughnut, the tender Oly-koek, and the crisp and crumbling cruller; sweet cakes and short cakes and ginger cakes. And then there were apple pies and pumpkin pies, besides slices of hams and smoked beef, and moreover delectable dishes of preserved plums and peaches and pears and quinces; not to mention fried shad and roasted chickens; together with bowls of milk and cream all mingled together higgledy-piggledy . . . with the motherly teapot sending up its clouds of vapor."

The English had no Santa Claus, that charming character being introduced by the Germans and Dutch. But the vigorous Christmas gradually triumphed over the early New England suspicion.

The Star

Mary had come
By ways so far,
And borne Him by
That brilliant star,
She found His face
Outshone by far
Day's burning sun
And night's great star.

Christmas Over the Continent

hristmas Eve was chosen by General Washington because the Hessians at Trenton were having their usual party. Surprised, they readily surrendered. The next Christmas was spent in misery at Valley Forge, the shelter huts unfinished, men sleeping on the frozen ground. The problem of keeping Christmas was solved with ingenuity. A squad from each brigade was sent out with wagons to forage among the farmers in the area, and enough gathered to give the men a decent dinner. The views of the contributing farmers are not known.

But in later years Christmas was a great day for General Washington.

At Mount Vernon, in the peace of his own home, Washington had a spirited Christmas with gifts, for all servants and slaves, and dancing at night.

In 1795 a certain Theophilus Bradbury wrote of Christmas dinner with President Washington in Philadelphia. He was with the "Vice-President, the Senators, the Delegates of Massachusetts, and some other members of Congress, about 20 in all . . . There was an elegant variety of roast beef, veal, turkeys, ducks, fowls, hams, etc.; puddings, jellies, oranges, apples, nuts, almonds, figs, raisins, and a variety of wines and punch . . . No lady but Mrs. Washington dined with us."

The American South had none of the New England coldness toward Christmas. They celebrated it more in the old English style, gaily, with hunting, drinking and surviving customs out of England. The Yule log was brought in and burned (soaked in water by the servants so that it would burn longer, as they were given as many days holiday as the log lasted). The Yule log was always ignited with a piece of the previous year's log.

The Moravians held a "love feast" the day before Christmas, women in black gowns and white caps, and men in dark clothes, served refreshments, after which the children were given each a lighted candle, to signify the Light that came to Bethlehem years before.

Even New England began to lose its austerity toward Christmas. By 1845 Boston was offering a variety of entertainments. At the Lyceum, you could hear, on the evening of December 25, Ralph Waldo Emerson lecture on the mystic Swedenborg. At the Melodeon hall, Handel's "The Messiah" was presented; tickets, fifty cents. At famed Fanueil Hall the National Anti-Slavery Bazaar was being held. At the Boston Museum, Cinderella was being presented for twenty-five cents.

In 1804 the Lewis and Clark expedition wintered among the Mandan villages on the Missouri River in Dakota country. Clark notes that on Christmas morning he was wakened by guns fired from three platoons of men and the French with them. Clark gave them "Taffia," fired three cannon, and raised the flag. Some men hunted, some danced.

Christmas for Lewis and Clark was miserable the next year. Having crossed the continent, they were near the mouth of the Columbia River. Again shooting woke them.

Clark then noted in his Journal: "After brackfast we divided our Tobacco . . . to those who doe not use it we make a present of a handkerchief. The Indians leave us in the evening. I recved a present of Cap. L. of fleece hosrie

Shirt Draws and Socks, a p Mockersons of Whitehouse . . . two Dozen white weazils tails of the Indian woman . . . we would have Spent this day the nativity of Christ in feasting, had we any thing either to raise our Sperits or even gratify our appetites, our Diner concisted of pore Elk, so much spoiled that we ate it thro' mear necessity. Some Spoiled pounded fish and a fiew roots."

At the same time, Zebulon M. Pike was near the source of the Mississippi. His journal notes that he "gave out two pounds of extra meat, two pounds of extra flour, one gill of whiskey, and some tobacco per man, in order to distinguish Christmas Day."

Next year, while seeking the source of the Arkansas River in Colorado, Pike and his men almost starved, having only a little buffalo meat without salt, which was eaten, however, with "generall content." Some years later at the same place an explorer was invited to eat with one of the "arrapaho Cheefs He seet before us a dish of fat meat of Which We Eat plentyfully." The "Cheef" then announced joyfully that the Christmas dinner had been a dog, a great delicacy with them.

Probably the first Christmas celebration by men coming west over the Appalachians was held in the Ohio country by Christopher Gist, who assembled a tribe of Indians and read the Christmas service of the Church of England. This was interpreted to the tribe, along with the assurance that it was the true faith which the King recommended to his children.

Gist recorded that "The Indians seemed well pleased, and came up to Me and returned Me their Thanks; and then invited me to live among Them."

By the middle of the nineteenth century Christmas was well established on this continent wherever white men had settled. It was very much in its modern form, the use of Santa Claus and the decorated tree having spread widely.

In the Southwest and in Catholic Canada there was usually a midnight mass on Christmas Eve. In the one area the local customs were Spanish, and in the other French.

It is likely that the first Christmas tree salesman was Mark Carr who, in 1851, in the Catskills, cut down two sled loads of fir and spruce, hauled them to the Hudson River and thence down to New York City. There he rented a strip of sidewalk at the corner of Vesey and Greenwich streets for one dollar. To his delight the project was tremendously successful, but he returned home broke, having spent his fine earnings on cheerful living.

Christmas was celebrated with a great deal more vigor in the new western settlements than in the traditionally reserved New England states. A true account of early Indianapolis relates that there was much dancing, jigs, reels, "puncheon splitters" and "hoedowns."

There was also "gander pulling." A tough old gander had its neck stripped of feathers and greased and was then strung up by the legs to a tree limb. The young men would gallop by and try to grab the greased neck and pull the gander loose. The risk there, of course, was that you might win the stringy old bird.

The Civil War brought its own Christmas problems. One of the most remarkable women involved in the war was Phoebe Yates Pember, matron of the Chimborazo Hospital in Richmond, largest on either side.

In 1863 she wrote: "It seemed to me I lived a week during the 24 hours which constituted Christmas . . . We made 24 gallons of Egg-Nogg inviting *all* in the whole Division to come and drink and gave to each a good sized cake. At two o'clock having roasted a dozen turkeys and seven gallons of oysters we shared them out and hoped that each man got his share. After all this was accomplished, I had the kitchen table carried into my little room, a personal turkey with all new accompaniaments sett out and then sent for the poor outcast Marylanders to come and dine . . ."

One Confederate soldier sold his $25 watch for $75, noting that "This sufficed for fuel for a month, and a Christmas dinner." By 1863 all food was outrageously expensive, turkeys having gone from $11 to $50, sorghum rum for eggnog going from $30 a gallon to $80. One dinner, a last despairing gesture of cheer in 1864, had a ham worth $300, a turkey $175, with coffee from sweet potatoes. At another Christmas dinner the host remarked sadly, "Our circle was small, but pleasant. The Christmas turkey and ham were not."

The vitality and emotional quality of Christmas survived every aspect of the American experience, and often must have given heart to people who were homesick, frightened and cold. Some ate dog; some ate bear, deer, beef, huckleberries.

For all, the strength lay not so much in food as in the animating childlike spirit of the season. For men and women sharing in the birth of a new country, to celebrate the birth of a Child was an act not only of faith but of assurance.

The Wise Men

Seeing that star,
The Wise Men, swift
To bow to the Boy,
Gave Him their gift.

Their gift was gold,
And the bent knee,
Hard metal and
Humility.

Now He, the son
Of Joseph's wife,
Gives then *His* gift:
Immortal life.

This is the hope
Of a world gone wild:
When proud men kneel
To a little Child.

Catholic Christmas in Early America

anada had none of the New England Puritan's denial of the right to praise Christmas with joy and festivity. It is recorded that in Quebec, 1645, music was provided on Christmas Eve by a bass singer, a violin and a German flute. A little cannon was fired as a signal that midnight mass was to begin. The wooden chapel was heated by four huge iron kettles which had fires built in them. One became so hot that it caused a fire in the floor under it, which was put out by a cook, he being most skilled with pots and kettles.

In the whole long extent of the Colonial Atlantic coast line during the seventeenth century, there was only one small area in which a true Roman Catholic Christmas could be observed. This was Maryland, which for over half of that century was a place of tolerance.

Father Andrew White came to establish a mission among the Indians, but unlike the fortunate French Jesuits among the Hurons in Canada, he had to abandon his work after what seemed like initial success.

The quick failure of the mission to the Indians was not repeated among the white Catholic worshipers of Maryland, who continued the same observances of the holiday as they had practiced in England. This was a cheerful Christmas, in contrast to the repudiation of the holiday by the Puritans at Plymouth, who celebrated their first Christmas in the New World by rigidly *not* celebrating.

The zeal for religion was so strong among the priests of Maryland that they actually went to Virginia, where Catholicism was not practiced, and bought the remaining time of certain indentured men so that they could come and worship in their own way. Only here was the Christmas mass heard on that wilderness coast.

The first Christmas ever observed in the New World was probably that of the French explorer, Jacques Cartier, in 1535, at what was later to become Quebec.

Cartier had praised the land in letters sent to France, describing its fertility and its promise for settlement. He built a fort close by his ships, but by Christmas four feet of snow had fallen, and scurvy had broken out among his men until they were too weak to appear.

The Indians, at first friendly, turned hostile, so that when they approached, the sick men had to shout and pound in a pathetic effort to seem strong enough to defend themselves. What was worse, their "drinkables" were frozen in the casks, so that they had only water and melted snow for comfort when racked with illness.

The first recorded mention of Christmas caroling on the American Continent occurs in a report of the Jesuit Father Bartholomew Vimont, dated Quebec, 1645. A good many Christian converts had been made among the Huron Indians, and Father Vimont describes their special zeal in celebrating Christmas. Even in the most remote mission of New France at Mackinac (Mackinaw, Michigan), he said:

"The savages have a particular devotion for the night that was enlightened by the birth of the Son of God. There was not one who refused to fast on the day that preceded it. They built a small chapel of cedar and fir branches in honor of the manger of the infant Jesus. They wished to perform some penance for better receiving Him into their hearts on that holy day, and even those who were at a distance of two days' journey met at a given place to *sing hymns in honor of the newborn Child* . . . Neither the inconvenience of the snow nor the severity of the cold could stifle the ardor of their devotion."

The first Christmas hymn written in the New World was an adaptation of a sixteenth-century French folk song, translated into the Huron language by the saintly Jesuit missionary, Father John de Brebeuf.

In 1649 this learned and brave man was tortured to death by the Iroquois in a prolonged and horrible manner, with hot hatchet heads. The hymn he taught his Christian converts was preserved by those Hurons who escaped the bloody massacre. It was set down by Father Etienne de Villeneuve under the title *Jesous Ahatonnia* (Jesus Is Born).

One problem of putting the words into the Huron language was that it had no letter *M,* so that the French diphthong *ou* was substituted. The name of the Virgin Mary was thus written "Ouraie" and pronounced "Warie."

It is touching to think of Brebeuf struggling to find a proper way for expressing with dignity, in a difficult and unwieldy savage tongue, while living crudely in a menacing wilderness, the old French phrases for the announcement of the birth of Christ by singing angels. (The initial phrase "O, harken to the angels' word" when translated read: "Aloki ekwatatennonten shekwachiendaen.")

It is stated that the Indians were so enthusiastic about singing in their own language, to French airs, at Christmas, that the priests allowed them to go on singing the same songs until Easter.

In the Spanish-speaking Southwest, one of the traditional ceremonies was the backyard performance of *Los Pastores* (The Shepherds), a curious mixture of medieval and contemporary details.

At one end of the yard a crude altar was built of boards, with steps, covered with black sateen. Here the manger scene was made from little objects of value or prettiness, such as Christmas cards, tinsel, a pincushion in a golden slipper, statues of the patron saint of every member of the family. The image of the Christ Child, a life-size doll, was placed on a pile of gaudy Christmas candies. Figures of cows, sheep and donkeys were added, and the Star of Bethlehem was fixed to the top of the altar.

At the other end of the yard would be a tent, sometimes with a bonfire before it, representing hell. The play would begin with a girl in white, with paper wings, pacing about reciting verses. Then shepherds would appear, carrying crooks elaborately decorated and wearing tin swords. From the tent of hell, sinister devils would rush out, six in black with masks of animals, and one dressed in red with a forked tail, representing Lucifer.

The good shepherds fought the evil devils and drove them back. Then an Indian rushed in, to be beaten back, only to charge again and again be beaten back. On this third attempt he was allowed to reach the image of the Child and kiss its foot.

Sometimes one of the shepherds would lie down, exhausted with the long journey, and when urged to go on would ask that the Babe be brought to him. Finally he would arise and accompany the others to the altar, when candy would be distributed to all the people.

Comedy relief was provided by a hermit, wearing a long gray robe with moss and the mask of an old man with a white beard. All went to the altar and knelt. The play was often given for many days in various parts of such places as the Mexican area of San Antonio.

At St. Genevieve, in Missouri, there would be a procession of choir boys and girls, dressed in white and carrying gold and silver crosses. The image of the infant Jesus would be borne in a satin-covered cradle with candles on either side. This was placed in a straw-filled manger at one end of the church, to the accompaniment of music.

As far as is known, the first Nativity pageant in New England was performed in the German Catholic church of the Holy Trinity in Boston, Christmas, 1851. The children of the parish, dressed as Oriental shepherds, carrying bundles of food, linen and other gifts, went in procession to the crib before the altar, singing Christmas carols. They left their gifts by the crib; these were later distributed to the poor. In their colorful costumes, hands folded, the children then marched away from the church.

The scene deserved such admiration that it had to be twice repeated for the benefit of Protestants as well as Catholics.

From the barbarous wilderness of sixteenth-century Canada, to the lush landscape of Maryland and the desert sand and rock of New Mexico, in the city and at sea, the power of Christmas has been so great on this continent that it has repeated its great act of dedication, praise and delight even against the most terrible obstacles. Wherever men went in this immense and unknown country, a little Child led them, and they never failed to present their gift and gratitude to Him.

The Yearly Birth

Now on this falling world
We sit and watch new hate
Fall on our face and hands.
Yet still we celebrate

An old event of love
With radiant hands and face.
We praise an ancient Child
And the harsh desert place,

That barn where He was born
Of woman, to defy
Worn winter's yearly death
With His first living cry.

Each time we praise that birth,
We—women, children, men—
Refresh our life in His.
We too are born again.

Christmas on the Moon

On the night of Christ's birth the great sign was a star moving in radiance across the sky. Out of the infinite darkness of the heavens it pointed to a rude barn in a small village surrounded by a country of wandering shepherds. It is important to note that Christ drew his first breath in a building already given over to animals and the sustaining of life.

Now the sky glows with satellites wandering across it, making their little radio sounds like metal sheep running over a predictable course and bleating. They are tremendous triumphs of human ingenuity. And they prove once again what a marvelously intelligent man has been given life on this Earth.

Yet clever as they are, the messages they send back are objective data about temperature, air density, radiation. They are as impersonal in their metal and ceramic shells as if they were made of stone.

The message coming from that original star was warm and immediate. It disclosed a living Child, and it said, "In Him was life; and the life was the Light of Men. . . . That was the true Light, which lighteth every man that cometh into the world."

Is it really progress when the gleaming object in our sky is not the sign of the immortal Child, but a miniature tape recorder or a pathetic dead dog? Is it any more meaningful in human terms when a superbly trained man sweeps in grand arcs through space?

Suppose the astonishing event happens, and men do land on the moon, wading about in that frothy dust and looking into the deep craters or up at the desolate, dead mountains. As they trudge slowly along they will be in constant radio communication with Earth, sending back reports on the observations made on their instruments, and receiving messages in return.

Suddenly into the flow of reception from Earth comes a phrase which makes no sense at all. Thinking it is only an error they continue their study of moon environment.

Then abruptly one man stops, surprised, doubtful, afraid to give in to his pleasure at the possible meaning of what he hears. Then another man stops. Soon the entire party is clustered in a circle, looking curiously at each other and listening to the radio from Earth.

There it comes again, clear, unmistakable, shocking in its emotional nostalgia. In the middle of the transmission of scientific information come the cheerful words, *"Merry Christmas."* In their deep concentration at being on that mad moon landscape, the men had forgotten the holiday back home.

They look at each other in uneasy quiet. In their carefully calculated time schedule, no allowance had been made for such an apparently frivolous interruption. One man shrugs his shoulders and starts on. Suddenly the first to stop speaks into the radio communicating with the other. With deliberate calm, as if he were giving an instrument reading, he says, "Merry Christmas."

They all look rapidly at each other and the one who had started walking stops, then comes toward them, and as he moves he shouts into his own microphone, "Merry Christmas, everybody." The group all then start calling the same old magical words until the thin air crackles with their cries.

By now it is evening and Earth has darkened. Without speaking of it, they all turn toward the live planet from which they had come, and each stares at what must be either a remarkable thing, or a pure and wished-for illusion.

It seems as if that western portion of Earth where the Christian countries are has begun to glow, as myriads of tiny lights come on in many colors. Each man again looks at the others, in doubt, in amazement, and in homesickness. The countless little lights of Christmas may not show at such a distance but are visible, even if only in their mortal eyes.

They had prepared for this trip over a long period of time. They had been physically, intellectually and emotionally conditioned for the strain of space travel. They were ready, it seemed, for separation from family as well as absence from the familiar Earth.

Yet two small words, as common as any in the language, childhood words, the most unscientific in the language, had broken up all of that sensible planning. The precise mind had given way to the feeling heart.

Each man remembers, with longing which is like an ache in his imagining eyes, the look of his home in the region to which he belongs.

The New Englander thinks of the white church tower rising in a purity of aspiration above the white snow, and sees children sliding on the rock-fenced hills, or men and women skiing on the low mountain slopes where evergreens bless the smooth surface with a laying-on of shadows. Across the common, families are walking to a church from whose windows light falls in a yellow splendor.

Southerners think of the blueness of distance in that mild air, the jack pine woods green over the red earth, the dun fields emptied now of cotton and tobacco. In the tradition of some parts of the South, firecrackers are exploding and children are exploding into streets at the gay sound. Holly is cut and hanging from the door.

The Middle Westerners recall the towns where lamp-posts are decorated with twisting lengths of green and lights arch over the street between rows of buildings which oddly mingle Civil War facades with contemporary glass. They visualize that countryside which is almost never flat, but forever slightly pitching and rolling, broken with groves of trees whose branches, bare of leaves, scrape the wind blowing through them, for this is not evergreen country. Yard lights glitter on farmyards where walking back and forth from house to barn to corncrib has worn dark paths in the snow. Or it is Chicago, Cleveland, Milwaukee, frozenly crowded with people along the frozen lake edge.

Men from the Southwest think of the hand-rubbed adobe churches growing out of the desert like natural things. Westerners think back to the Rockies or Sierras under their immense snows, the villages burning small lights on which the hymns seem to make their tiny sound against the overwhelming silence.

For West Coast men, it is that sparkling length of sand and surf running along the Pacific beach from Mexico to Canada. And the Canadians have their own beautiful variety, from the French-speaking towns of Quebec, the huddled seashore villages on the Atlantic islands, to the prairie churches rising out of the wide fields where wheat yellowed in summer.

No matter where they are from they think of children bubbling with the eagerness of the season. The marvelous achievement of mind which put them on that childless place has brought not only a new increase of knowledge, but a repetition of the oldest, simplest emotion they can have—homesickness to be home on Christmas Eve. They look at each other and smile, thinking, perhaps, of the amusing legend of the mistletoe.

In that dead atmosphere, it is the celebration of a Child's birth which brings them back to the living Earth. They go back to work, renewed, and glad to be human creatures who feel as well as think.